# Offshore Fishing Adventures

**Hooked On Reel Fishing**

Michael Clutton

Published by Michael Clutton, 2024.

While every precaution has been taken in the preparation of this book, the publisher assumes no responsibility for errors or omissions, or for damages resulting from the use of the information contained herein.

OFFSHORE FISHING ADVENTURES

**First edition. June 30, 2024.**



ISBN: 979-8224056057

Written by Michael Clutton.

# Table of Contents

# Offshore Fishing Adventures: Hooked on Reel Fishing

# Offshore Fishing Adventures

Ahoy there, fellow anglers and curious landlubbers! Welcome to the wild, wonderful, and occasionally wacky world of offshore fishing. Whether you're here to wrestle big marlins or simply got lost in the bookstore, we're happy you're joining us on this fishy adventure. Get ready to explore a vast, enigmatic knowledge sea. We promise to reel you in with tales, tips, and trivia that are more entertaining than a school of dancing sardines.

**Overview of Offshore Fishing**

Offshore fishing, sometimes referred to as deep-sea fishing, is the ultimate aquatic adventure. It's a challenging and exciting type of fishing that takes place in the open ocean, where the water is deep and the fish is large. Unlike freshwater fishing, offshore fishing lets you catch big fish like tuna, marlin, and swordfish that you won't find in local ponds. It's about pitting your wits against some of nature's most formidable creatures and enjoying the journey as much as the catch.

## Why Deep Sea Fishing?

Now, you might wonder, "Why do people get hooked on offshore fishing?" Well, for starters, it's the perfect blend of serenity and adrenaline. Picture this: You're lounging on a boat, sun on your face, cold drink in hand, when suddenly—BAM!—your reel spins, and you're in a tug-of-war with a beast of the deep. It's like going from a meditative yoga session to a WWE wrestling match in the blink of an eye.

There's also the bragging rights. Let's face it, anyone can catch a trout, but it takes a true hero (or a fortunate novice) to land a 500-pound marlin. And let's not forget the stories. Offshore fishing gives you endless stories, from slightly exaggerated to unbelievable. The idea of tapping into your inner Hemingway is appealing, even if you haven't been near the ocean before.

So, gear up, because we're about to set sail on an epic quest for knowledge, adventure, and possibly, the best fish puns you've ever heard.

# 1 - Essential Gear and Equipment

## Hook, Line, and Sinker

Imagine this: you're out on the sparkling blue ocean, the sun gleaming, birds chirping overhead, and the invigorating smell of salt in the air. You've spent a lot on fancy fishing gear, like a high-tech rod, gold reel, and a practical vest with lots of storage. You're feeling invincible, the master angler ready to catch the big one. There's just one minor problem—you forgot the bait.

This is exactly what happened to Bob Simmons, a seasoned fisherman from Gulf Shores, Alabama, known for his meticulous attention to detail. One breezy Saturday morning in June 1992, Bob set out with his friends for a much-anticipated deep-sea fishing trip. He had spent weeks preparing, ensuring every piece of equipment was top-notch. His friends were impressed by his shiny new gear, and Bob couldn't wait to show them up with the biggest catch of the day.

As they anchored at a prime fishing spot, Bob confidently reached for his bait cooler, ready to rig his line and make the first cast. To his horror, he found the cooler empty. In his excitement, Bob had left his carefully prepared bait at home, sitting on the kitchen counter. His heart sank, and a sheepish grin spread across his face as he turned to his friends.

The laughter erupted instantly. Bob's friends were laughing so hard that they almost fell overboard. Bob, always the good sport, couldn't help but chuckle along with them, despite his embarrassment. His high-tech rod, gold-plated reel, and tactical fishing vest were rendered utterly useless without the humble bait.

Determined not to let the day go to waste, Bob improvised with bits of lunch leftovers and even tried fashioning makeshift lures from pieces of his tackle box. Needless to say, the fish weren't biting. His friends, still chuckling, caught a few decent-sized fish, while Bob's line remained frustratingly empty.

The moral of the story? Always double-check your gear, folks. No amount of fancy equipment can replace the basics. Bob's fishing story became a hit with his friends, proving that even experienced anglers can forget important things. And Bob? He learned to keep a checklist, ensuring that every future trip included the all-important bait.

### Overview of Necessary Equipment

To successfully embark on an offshore fishing adventure, you need to be equipped with more than just enthusiasm. Here's a rundown of essential gear:

**Rods and Reels**

- **Rods**: Choose rods based on the type of fish you're targeting. For offshore fishing, a heavy-duty rod is essential.
- **Reels**: Pair your rod with a strong, corrosion-resistant reel. Offshore reels are built to handle the pressure of deep-sea fishing.

**Bait and Tackle**

- **Bait**: Live bait such as squid, mullet, or sardines can attract a variety of fish. Artificial lures are also a must.
- **Tackle**: Include hooks, lines, sinkers, swivels, and leaders in your tackle box.

**Safety Gear**

- **Life Jackets**: Never underestimate the importance of a good life jacket.
- **First Aid Kit**: A well-stocked first aid kit is crucial for dealing with minor injuries.
- **Communication Devices**: Ensure you have a reliable VHF radio and a backup communication device.

**Additional Gear**

- **Fishing License**: Make sure you have the necessary permits.
- **Coolers**: Essential for keeping your catch fresh.
- **Sun Protection**: Hats, sunscreen, and sunglasses to protect against the elements.

**Fresh Bait**

1. **The Bamboo Rod**: The first fishing rods were made from bamboo, which is still favored by some purists today for its flexibility and

strength.

2.  **Reel Evolution**: The fishing reel dates back to the 4th century China, initially used for storing line rather than casting.
3.  **Synthetic Lines**: Modern fishing lines are often made from braided synthetics like Dyneema, offering superior strength and durability.
4.  **Deep-sea Lures**: Some lures are designed to mimic bioluminescent sea creatures, attracting fish in the dark depths.
5.  **Stainless Steel Hooks**: These hooks are popular due to their resistance to corrosion in saltwater environments.
6.  **Electric Reels**: High-tech electric reels can automatically adjust drag and retrieve line, making deep-sea fishing more efficient.
7.  **The Penn Reel**: Penn, a prominent reel manufacturer, has been a staple in the industry since 1932, known for their high-quality saltwater reels.
8.  **Circle Hooks**: Invented by ancient Polynesians, circle hooks are designed to hook fish in the corner of the mouth, reducing injury.
9.  **Monofilament Line**: Introduced in the 1950s, monofilament lines revolutionized fishing due to their affordability and ease of use.
10. **Portable Fish Finders**: Modern anglers use sophisticated sonar devices to locate fish schools beneath the surface.
11. **Carbon Fiber Rods**: These rods are incredibly strong yet lightweight, perfect for battling big game fish.
12. **The Alvey Reel**: An Australian invention, the Alvey sidecast reel is beloved for its simplicity and ruggedness.
13. **Baitcasting Reels**: Known for their precision, baitcasting reels are a favorite among experienced anglers targeting larger species.
14. **Fluorocarbon Leaders**: These leaders are nearly invisible underwater, making them perfect for wary fish.
15. **Hydraulic Outriggers**: These devices extend fishing lines away from the boat, allowing for more lines to be trolled simultaneously.
16. **Drift Sock**: A tool used to slow down the boat's drift, ensuring a more controlled fishing experience in windy conditions.
17. **Jigging Master**: A brand known for its high-end jigging rods and reels, essential for targeting bottom-dwelling fish.
18. **Kayak Fishing**: A growing trend where anglers use specially equipped kayaks to reach fishing spots boats can't access.

19. **Barometer Watches**: These watches help anglers predict fish activity based on atmospheric pressure changes.
20. **Fish Grippers**: Handy tools for safely handling large, toothy fish without risking fingers.

## Detailed Descriptions and Uses
## Rods

- **Heavy-duty Rods**: These rods are essential for offshore fishing due to their ability to handle large, powerful fish. They are typically longer and sturdier than freshwater rods.

## Reels

- **Offshore Reels**: Built to withstand the harsh conditions of saltwater, these reels are designed with corrosion-resistant materials and powerful drag systems to battle big game fish.

## Bait and Tackle

- **Live Bait**: Squid, mullet, and sardines are effective in attracting a wide range of fish species.
- **Artificial Lures**: Designed to mimic the appearance and movement of prey, these lures come in various shapes, sizes, and colors to target specific fish.

## Safety Gear

- **Life Jackets**: A non-negotiable piece of equipment, life jackets provide buoyancy and increase survival chances in case of an accident.
- **First Aid Kit**: Includes bandages, antiseptics, and other essentials for treating minor injuries.

## Frozen Bait

1. **High-Tech Reels**: Some modern electric reels can cost over $3,000,

featuring digital displays and programmable functions.

2. **Fishing Line Strength**: The strongest fishing line, made from braided synthetics, can hold up to 200 pounds.
3. **Record-Breaking Rods**: The longest fishing rod on record measures a staggering 59 feet and 5 inches.
4. **Ancient Hooks**: The oldest known fishing hooks, made from shell, date back to 23,000 years ago.
5. **Sonar Accuracy**: Advanced fish finders can detect schools of fish up to 3,000 feet below the surface.

## Maintenance and Care Tips

- **Rinse After Use**: Always rinse your rods, reels, and tackle with fresh water after each use to remove salt and prevent corrosion.
- **Regular Inspections**: Check your gear for signs of wear and tear, such as frayed lines, rusted hooks, and loose fittings.
- **Proper Storage**: Store your rods vertically to prevent bending, and keep reels in a cool, dry place to avoid damage from humidity.
- **Lubrication**: Regularly lubricate reel components to ensure smooth operation and longevity.
- **Hook Care**: Sharpen hooks periodically and replace any that are bent or corroded.

By keeping your gear in top condition, you'll ensure that each fishing trip is as successful and enjoyable as possible. So remember, whether you're a seasoned pro or a weekend warrior, your gear is your best friend out on the open sea—treat it well!

# 2 - Fundamentals and Techniques

**Hook, Line, and Sinker**

Imagine this: Jerry Thompson, a fisherman from Key West, Florida, decided one sunny morning in July 1985 to try catching a marlin. Jerry was known around the marina for his impressive fishing tales, albeit with a slight tendency to forget crucial items. On this day, he was so excited about the perfect weather and calm seas that he hurriedly loaded his gear onto his boat and set off without realizing he had left all his bait at home.

Determined not to let a little thing like that ruin his day, Jerry docked his boat about 10 miles offshore, right over a promising marlin hotspot. As he rummaged through his tackle box, the horrifying realization hit him: no bait. His heart sank. But Jerry wasn't one to give up easily. He searched his pockets for anything useful and found nothing but an old, crumpled gum wrapper. He unwrapped the piece of gum, chewed it absentmindedly, and stared at the shiny foil wrapper.

With a shrug and a prayer, Jerry fashioned the gum wrapper into a makeshift lure, tying it to his hook in a way that it fluttered like a tiny silver fish. He cast his line into the deep blue sea, chuckling at his own desperation but secretly hoping for a miracle. To his surprise, the reflective wrapper glinted and danced in the water, catching the attention of a nearby marlin.

Much to everyone's astonishment, an hour later, Jerry was battling a feisty marlin. It was a spectacular fight, the kind that draws a crowd and cements a fisherman's reputation. As Jerry wrestled with the giant fish, other boats circled around to watch the unexpected showdown. The marlin leaped and splashed, seemingly baffled by the odd bait but nonetheless hooked.

After an intense battle, Jerry managed to reel in the marlin, its impressive size drawing gasps and cheers from the onlookers. As he hoisted his catch, he couldn't help but laugh at the absurdity of the situation. Jerry's victory wasn't just about skill; it was a testament to ingenuity, a lot of luck, and perhaps the marlin's poor taste in snacks.

The story of Jerry and his gum wrapper lure quickly became legend in Key West, a favorite tale retold at every local bar and bait shop. It reminded everyone that sometimes, even in the world of fishing, creativity and a little bit of madness can lead to the most remarkable catches.

**Basic Techniques and Methods**

**Trolling**

Trolling involves dragging baited lines or lures behind a moving boat. It's effective for covering large areas and targeting pelagic fish like tuna, marlin, and mahi-mahi.

**Jigging**

Jigging uses a weighted lure, often resembling a fish or squid, which is jerked vertically through the water. This technique is excellent for enticing bottom-dwelling fish like snapper and grouper.

**Bottom Fishing**

Bottom fishing targets fish that live on or near the sea floor. This method uses heavy weights to keep baited hooks close to the bottom, ideal for catching species like halibut and cod.

**Fresh Bait**

**Juicy Tidbits About Offshore Fishing Techniques**

1. **Ancient Trolling**: The ancient Greeks were known to practice trolling, using a trailing line behind their ships to catch fish while traveling.
2. **Vertical Jigging**: Originating in Japan, vertical jigging became popular in the 20th century and is particularly effective in deep waters.
3. **Chumming**: This technique involves dispersing ground bait (chum) to attract fish to the boat, first recorded in the early 1900s.
4. **The Downrigger**: Invented in the 1930s, downriggers allow anglers to troll baits at specific depths, revolutionizing offshore fishing.
5. **Fly Fishing at Sea**: While typically a freshwater technique, saltwater fly fishing began gaining popularity in the 1960s.
6. **Kite Fishing**: Developed in China, kite fishing allows baits to be presented on the water's surface, ideal for targeting surface feeders.
7. **Tuna Towers**: Introduced in the 1950s, these elevated platforms on boats help anglers spot schools of tuna from a distance.
8. **Deep Dropping**: This method uses electric reels to drop bait to extreme depths (over 300 meters) to catch species like swordfish.
9. **Spearfishing**: Ancient and effective, spearfishing has been used for

thousands of years, with modern techniques employing underwater guns.

10. **The "Greenstick" Method**: Originating in Japan, this technique uses long, flexible poles to suspend multiple lures and is effective for tuna.
11. **Sight Fishing**: This method relies on visually spotting fish before casting, often used in clear, shallow waters.
12. **Live Bait Bridling**: A technique where live bait is hooked in a way that allows it to swim naturally, increasing its appeal to predators.
13. **Planing Boards**: These devices help spread lines out to the sides of a boat, allowing for more lures to be trolled simultaneously.
14. **Bait and Switch**: A method where teasers attract fish close to the boat before live bait is presented to seal the deal.
15. **FADs (Fish Aggregating Devices)**: These man-made structures attract fish, making it easier for anglers to locate schools.
16. **Power Casting**: Using powerful rods and reels, anglers can cast heavy lures far offshore, targeting elusive species.
17. **Electronic Lures**: High-tech lures with LED lights and vibrating motors mimic the movement and appearance of prey.
18. **The "Stump Pull" Technique**: Used in bottom fishing, this method involves yanking the rod to dislodge fish from rocky areas.
19. **Light Tackle Offshore**: Using lighter gear in offshore fishing provides a more challenging and sporting experience.
20. **Night Fishing**: Many species are more active at night, making night fishing a popular technique for offshore anglers.

## Techniques for Success

- **Drift Fishing**: Use the natural movement of the boat to cover large areas without constantly reeling in lines.
- **Trolling Patterns**: Employ zig-zag or S-shaped trolling patterns to simulate the erratic movement of fleeing baitfish.
- **Bait Rigging**: Perfect your bait rigging skills to ensure baits swim naturally, increasing their attractiveness to predators.
- **Match the Hatch**: Use lures and baits that closely resemble the local prey species to increase your chances of a bite.

- **Fish Aggregating Devices**: Seek out FADs to find concentrated schools of fish, particularly pelagic species.

## Frozen Bait

1. **Deep Dropping Depths**: Some deep-dropping techniques target depths up to 6,000 feet, using specialized equipment to handle the pressure.
2. **Trolling Speed**: Optimal trolling speeds vary by species but generally range from 5 to 9 knots, depending on the target fish.
3. **Record Jigging Catch**: The largest fish caught using a jigging technique was a 506-pound bluefin tuna.
4. **Chumming Success**: Studies have shown that chumming can increase fish catch rates by up to 300%.
5. **Electric Reels**: High-end electric reels can cost over $2,000 and are equipped with features like line counters and programmable drag settings.

## Common Mistakes and How to Avoid Them

1. **Overcomplicating Techniques**: Keep it simple. Focus on mastering basic techniques before moving on to advanced methods.
   - **Tip**: Start with basic trolling and bottom fishing before experimenting with more complex techniques like kite fishing.
2. **Ignoring Local Knowledge**: Local anglers and guides have invaluable knowledge about specific fishing areas.
   - **Tip**: Take the time to learn from locals, and don't hesitate to ask for advice on best practices and hot spots.
3. **Inadequate Gear Maintenance**: Neglecting gear maintenance can lead to failures at critical moments.
   - **Tip**: Regularly inspect and maintain all equipment, and always have backup gear on hand.
4. **Improper Bait Presentation**: Even the best bait is useless if not presented correctly.
   - **Tip**: Practice rigging techniques to ensure your bait appears natural and

enticing to fish.

5. **Ignoring Weather and Tides**: Weather conditions and tides significantly impact fish behavior and safety.
    - **Tip**: Always check weather forecasts and tidal charts before heading out, and adjust your plans accordingly.

By understanding and mastering these fundamentals and techniques, you'll be well on your way to becoming a proficient offshore angler. Just remember, practice makes perfect, and there's always something new to learn out on the open water!

# 3 - Types of Offshore Fishing

**Hook, Line, and Sinker**

In the summer of 1967, an eccentric fisherman named Captain Gus O'Malley became a legend in the coastal town of Rockport, Maine. Gus, a retired navy man with a penchant for quirky improvisation, decided to try his hand at spearfishing one hot August afternoon. Unfortunately, he couldn't find his trusty spear—apparently loaned to a neighbor who promised to return it "soon." Never one to be deterred by minor inconveniences, Gus grabbed the next best thing he could find: his old garden rake, a rusty tool he'd used for years in his vegetable patch.

With a wry smile, Gus tied the rake to a sturdy pole with some old rope, creating what he dubbed "the sea rake." Armed with his makeshift contraption, Captain Gus donned his snorkeling gear and waded into the water, much to the amusement of onlookers gathered at the dock.

As Gus paddled out to a promising spot near the kelp beds, he recalled his navy training and steeled himself for the task ahead. The sight was something to behold—an old sea dog, weathered by years at sea, wielding a garden rake with the enthusiasm of a seasoned gardener. Gus waved the implement around with surprisingly adept strokes, the rake tines glinting in the sunlight as they swept through the water.

Incredibly, after about half an hour of determined effort, Gus managed to snag a couple of fish. They were small, silver-scaled mackerels, but fish nonetheless. He also gathered a considerable amount of seaweed, which clung to the rake's tines like green confetti. As he emerged triumphantly from the water, dripping with both seawater and success, the crowd erupted in cheers and laughter. Captain Gus O'Malley's escapade quickly became legendary in Rockport, a testament to resourcefulness and perhaps a touch of madness.

The story of Captain Gus and his garden rake spread beyond Rockport, becoming a local legend and an enduring example of creativity and determination. To this day, old-timers at the Rockport Marina still chuckle about "Gus and the Sea Rake," a quirky chapter in the town's rich fishing history that highlights the ingenuity and humor of fishermen everywhere.

**Different Approaches and Styles**

**Sport Fishing**

Sport fishing is all about the thrill of the chase and the joy of the catch. Anglers target game fish like marlin, tuna, and sailfish, often releasing them after the catch.

**Commercial Fishing**

Commercial fishing focuses on harvesting large quantities of fish and seafood for sale and consumption. Methods include trawling, longlining, and purse seining, targeting species such as cod, haddock, and shrimp.

**Recreational Fishing**

Recreational fishing is a leisurely activity enjoyed by individuals and families. It includes various techniques, from trolling to bottom fishing, and often targets a variety of fish for fun rather than profit.

**Fresh Bait**

**Juicy Tidbits About Different Types of Offshore Fishing**

1. **Tuna Tournaments**: The first organized tuna fishing tournament was held in 1939 in Massachusetts, offering substantial cash prizes and fostering sport fishing camaraderie.
2. **Purse Seining Origins**: Purse seining, a method for capturing large schools of fish, has roots in ancient fishing techniques used by Native Americans.
3. **Longlining Legacy**: Longlining, where baited hooks are attached to a main line, dates back to ancient China and was documented as early as the 2nd century BC.
4. **Deep-Sea Diving**: Spearfishing with primitive equipment has been practiced for thousands of years, with ancient Greeks known for their free-diving spearfishing techniques.
5. **Recreational Revolution**: Recreational fishing gained popularity in the 19th century with the invention of lightweight fishing rods and reels.
6. **Commercial Trawling**: Trawling nets, used extensively in commercial fishing, were developed in the early 20th century to efficiently capture large quantities of fish.
7. **Catch and Release**: The concept of catch and release in sport fishing emerged in the mid-20th century as a conservation effort to maintain

fish populations.

8. **First Charter Boats**: The first fishing charters for sport fishing began in the 1920s in Florida, providing guided fishing trips for tourists.

9. **FADs Utilization**: Fish Aggregating Devices (FADs) have been used since the 1980s to attract pelagic fish and improve fishing yields.

10. **Trolling Innovation**: The downrigger, an essential tool for trolling at specific depths, was patented in the 1930s, enhancing sport fishing techniques.

11. **Drift Net History**: Drift nets, used in commercial fishing, date back to the 18th century and were originally made from natural fibers.

12. **Kayak Fishing**: Modern offshore kayak fishing emerged in the late 20th century, providing a new, eco-friendly approach to recreational fishing.

13. **Sonar in Fishing**: The introduction of sonar technology in the 1950s revolutionized both sport and commercial fishing by improving fish location accuracy.

14. **Fly Fishing for Tarpon**: Saltwater fly fishing for species like tarpon became popular in the 1960s, combining the skills of freshwater fly fishing with offshore adventure.

15. **Tuna Ranching**: Developed in the late 20th century, tuna ranching involves capturing young tuna and raising them in pens until they reach market size.

16. **Whale Fishing History**: Whaling, an early form of commercial fishing, dates back to the 11th century, though it has largely been replaced by conservation efforts.

17. **First Fishing Regulations**: The first fishing regulations to protect fish stocks were enacted in the 19th century, recognizing the need for sustainable practices.

18. **Game Fish Tagging**: Tagging programs for game fish, started in the 1950s, help researchers track fish movements and populations.

19. **Deep-Sea Spearfishing Competitions**: Competitive spearfishing tournaments began in the mid-20th century, showcasing the skills of divers worldwide.

20. **Eco-Tourism Fishing**: Eco-tourism fishing trips, which focus on sustainable practices and environmental education, have gained

popularity in recent decades.

## Benefits and Challenges of Each Type

### Sport Fishing

**Benefits**: Excitement of the catch, conservation through catch and release, camaraderie in tournaments. **Challenges**: High costs of equipment and charters, potential for long hours without a catch.

### Commercial Fishing

**Benefits**: Economic livelihood for communities, efficient harvesting methods, ability to supply large quantities of seafood. **Challenges**: Environmental impact, strict regulations, physical demands on fishers.

### Recreational Fishing

**Benefits**: Relaxation and leisure, accessibility for all skill levels, bonding with family and friends. **Challenges**: Requires patience and skill, can be affected by weather and environmental conditions.

### Frozen Bait

1. **Largest Tuna Caught**: The largest bluefin tuna ever caught weighed 1,496 pounds, highlighting the potential size of sport fishing targets.
2. **Commercial Fishing Fleet**: There are approximately 4.6 million fishing vessels worldwide, with commercial fishing boats making up the majority.
3. **Economic Impact**: Recreational fishing contributes over $125 billion annually to the U.S. economy, showcasing its significant economic role.
4. **Fish Consumption**: The average person consumes about 20 kilograms of fish per year, much of which is supplied by commercial fisheries.
5. **Sport Fishing Participation**: Over 49 million Americans participate in recreational fishing, making it one of the most popular outdoor activities in the country.

## Choosing the Right Method for You

### Personal Interest

- **Thrill Seekers**: Sport fishing is ideal for those who love adventure and the challenge of catching big game fish.

- **Economic Goals**: Commercial fishing is suitable for individuals or families looking to make a livelihood from the sea.
- **Leisurely Pursuits**: Recreational fishing is perfect for those seeking relaxation and a connection with nature.

## Budget

- **High-End**: Sport fishing can be expensive due to the cost of specialized gear and charter services.
- **Moderate to High**: Commercial fishing requires significant investment in boats and equipment but offers potential returns.
- **Variable**: Recreational fishing can be done on any budget, from basic shore fishing to more elaborate offshore trips.

## Location

- **Coastal Areas**: Ideal for all types of offshore fishing due to proximity to rich fishing grounds.
- **Urban Centers**: Accessible recreational fishing options like charter services are available, though may require travel for sport or commercial fishing.
- **Rural Locations**: Often provide easy access to prime fishing spots and may have a strong tradition of commercial fishing.

By understanding the different types of offshore fishing and their respective benefits and challenges, you can make an informed decision about which method suits you best. Whether you're in it for the thrill, the livelihood, or the relaxation, there's a style of offshore fishing that's just right for you. Happy fishing!

# 4 - Popular Locations and Hotspots

**Hook, Line, and Sinker**

Imagine this: Tom Parker, a weekend angler from the suburbs of Phoenix, decided to sharpen his skills before his big trip to the coast. Tom was known among his friends for his enthusiastic, albeit somewhat misguided, approach to hobbies. Fishing was his latest passion, and he was determined to be ready for his upcoming ocean fishing adventure.

One sunny Saturday afternoon in June 2012, Tom packed up his fishing gear and headed to the local community pool. He figured it was the perfect spot to practice casting and reeling, despite the obvious lack of oceanic fish. As he walked through the gates, his tackle box clanking, he ignored the puzzled stares of lifeguards and children splashing in the water. Undeterred, Tom found a spot at the edge of the pool, set up his gear, and began casting his line into the chlorinated water.

His aim? To practice catching tuna, naturally. With each cast, he envisioned the mighty tuna he hoped to hook on his coastal trip. The absurdity of the situation didn't faze him; Tom was focused, his eyes scanning the shimmering pool surface as if it were the deep blue sea.

As he continued his peculiar practice, lifeguards exchanged bemused glances, and kids giggled, whispering about the "crazy fisherman." Tom paid them no mind. Hours passed, and Tom's dedication never wavered. He reeled in his line time and time again, undeterred by the complete lack of fish.

Then, just as the sun began to dip, a tug on his line jolted Tom from his concentrated state. His heart raced as he imagined the battle with a giant tuna. He steadied himself, reeling with determination. Onlookers gathered, curious to see what the determined fisherman had hooked.

With a final heave, Tom triumphantly pulled his catch from the water—a waterlogged rubber ducky, its bright yellow paint faded from years of pool duty. Undeterred by the oddity of his catch, Tom declared it the "catch of the day," raising it high for all to see. The lifeguards applauded sarcastically, and the kids erupted in laughter, chanting, "Rubber Ducky!"

Tom's antics became an instant legend at the pool, a story retold with laughter and disbelief. Needless to say, Tom learned that real fishing requires a real ocean—and some common sense. His rubber ducky escapade, while not yielding any fish, did offer valuable lessons in preparation and humility.

When Tom finally made it to the coast, he was better prepared, not just with his gear but with a newfound appreciation for the unpredictable nature of fishing. His friends, hearing the pool story, couldn't help but tease him, but they also admired his unwavering spirit. Tom's story added a humorous chapter to his fishing journey, a reminder that sometimes, the best fishing tales are the ones where nothing goes quite as planned.

**Top Locations for Offshore Fishing**

**The Great Barrier Reef, Australia**

Renowned for its stunning biodiversity, the Great Barrier Reef is a top destination for anglers seeking marlin, tuna, and a variety of reef fish.

**Cabo San Lucas, Mexico**

Famous for its abundant marine life and picturesque coastline, Cabo San Lucas offers excellent fishing opportunities for marlin, dorado, and sailfish.

**Key West, Florida**

Known for its crystal-clear waters and diverse fish species, Key West is a prime spot for catching tarpon, sailfish, and snapper.

**Kona, Hawaii**

With its deep offshore waters, Kona is ideal for big game fishing, particularly for blue marlin, mahi-mahi, and yellowfin tuna.

**The Bahamas**

The Bahamas boast a variety of fishing environments, from deep-sea to flats fishing, where anglers can target bonefish, marlin, and wahoo.

**Prince Edward Island, Canada**

Famed for its giant bluefin tuna, Prince Edward Island attracts anglers from around the world looking to catch record-breaking tuna.

**Fresh Bait**

1. **The Great Barrier Reef**: The Great Barrier Reef is home to over 1,500 species of fish, making it a paradise for anglers.
2. **Cabo San Lucas**: Known as the "Marlin Capital of the World," Cabo hosts numerous fishing tournaments, including the famous Bisbee's Black & Blue.
3. **Key West**: Ernest Hemingway was an avid fisherman in Key West, and

his legacy is celebrated annually with the Hemingway Days festival and fishing tournament.

4. **Kona Coast**: The waters off Kona are exceptionally calm, creating perfect conditions for year-round big game fishing.

5. **The Bahamas**: Bimini in the Bahamas was a favorite fishing spot for writer Zane Grey, who helped popularize sport fishing there in the 1930s.

6. **Prince Edward Island**: The island holds the record for the largest bluefin tuna ever caught, weighing in at a staggering 1,496 pounds.

7. **Madeira, Portugal**: Known for its giant blue marlin, Madeira's waters have produced numerous world-record catches.

8. **Ascension Island**: Located in the South Atlantic Ocean, Ascension Island is renowned for its huge yellowfin tuna and blue marlin.

9. **Malindi, Kenya**: This location offers an incredible variety of game fish, including sailfish, marlin, and giant trevally.

10. **Bermuda**: The Bermuda Triple Crown Billfish Championship is one of the most prestigious billfish tournaments in the world.

11. **Canary Islands, Spain**: The waters around the Canary Islands are teeming with blue marlin, white marlin, and swordfish.

12. **Florida Keys**: The Florida Keys are home to the Seven Mile Bridge, a hotspot for tarpon fishing during the annual migration.

13. **Puerto Vallarta, Mexico**: Known for its diverse marine life, Puerto Vallarta is a hotspot for catching large yellowfin tuna.

14. **Cape Verde**: This archipelago is famed for its abundant blue marlin and has become a popular destination for big game fishing.

15. **Phuket, Thailand**: The Andaman Sea off Phuket offers anglers the chance to catch sailfish, barracuda, and giant trevally.

16. **Panama**: The Gulf of Chiriquí in Panama is renowned for its excellent fishing for marlin, sailfish, and roosterfish.

17. **Seychelles**: The waters around the Seychelles islands are rich with tuna, dorado, and wahoo, making it a prime fishing destination.

18. **San Diego, California**: San Diego is known for its fantastic offshore fishing, particularly for yellowtail, bluefin tuna, and dorado.

19. **Venice, Louisiana**: Known as the "Tuna Town," Venice offers some of the best tuna fishing in the Gulf of Mexico.

20. **Galápagos Islands, Ecuador**: The Galápagos are famous for their diverse marine life, including large schools of tuna and marlin.

## Seasonal and Regional Variations

- **Spring**: This is often the start of the fishing season in many regions, with species like marlin and sailfish becoming more active.
- **Summer**: Peak season for offshore fishing, with warm waters attracting big game fish like tuna, mahi-mahi, and marlin.
- **Fall**: As waters cool, fishing can remain excellent, particularly for species like wahoo and sailfish.
- **Winter**: In tropical and subtropical regions, winter can still offer great fishing, especially for species that thrive in cooler waters, such as sailfish and certain types of tuna.

## Regional Variations

- **Tropical Regions**: Offer year-round fishing due to consistent warm water temperatures.
- **Temperate Regions**: Have more defined fishing seasons, often influenced by migratory patterns and water temperatures.
- **Polar Regions**: Fishing seasons are short but can be highly productive, particularly for species adapted to cold waters.

## Frozen Bait

1. **Great Barrier Reef**: This iconic reef is visible from space and supports one of the world's most diverse marine ecosystems. It spans over 1,400 miles and is home to more than 1,500 species of fish.
2. **Cabo San Lucas**: Cabo's waters host the annual Los Cabos Billfish Tournament, which has awarded millions in prizes since its inception. The area is famed for its abundance of striped marlin.
3. **Key West**: The record for the largest tarpon caught in Key West is a whopping 243 pounds. Key West is also known for its vibrant coral reefs and shipwrecks, which attract a variety of marine life.

4.  **Kona Coast**: Kona is known for producing more grander marlins (over 1,000 pounds) than anywhere else in the world. The calm waters and deep drop-offs close to shore make it an ideal spot for big game fishing.
5.  **The Bahamas**: The waters around Bimini are so clear that divers can see up to 200 feet underwater on a good day. This clarity makes it a popular destination for both fishing and diving enthusiasts.

## Local Tips and Tricks
### Great Barrier Reef, Australia

- **Bait**: Live bait such as pilchards and squid work best.
- **Timing**: Early morning and late afternoon are prime times.
- **Regulations**: Always check local fishing regulations to protect the reef's delicate ecosystem.

### Cabo San Lucas, Mexico

- **Bait**: Trolled ballyhoo and live mackerel are popular choices.
- **Timing**: The peak fishing season runs from May to November.
- **Regulations**: Ensure you have the appropriate fishing licenses and are aware of the limits on catch sizes.

### Key West, Florida

- **Bait**: Use live shrimp or mullet for tarpon.
- **Timing**: Tarpon fishing is best during the spring migration from April to June.
- **Regulations**: Be mindful of size limits and protected species regulations.

### Kona, Hawaii

- **Bait**: Skipjack tuna and squid are effective for marlin.
- **Timing**: Year-round, but summer months are particularly good for big game fishing.

- **Regulations**: Follow local guidelines to ensure sustainable fishing practices.

## The Bahamas

- **Bait**: Live bait like pilchards or artificial lures.
- **Timing**: Marlin season peaks from March to June.
- **Regulations**: Adhere to local conservation laws to protect marine life.

## Seasonal and Regional Variations
## Seasonal Variations

- **Spring**: This is often the start of the fishing season in many regions, with species like marlin and sailfish becoming more active. Warmer water temperatures encourage more fish to move closer to shore.
- **Summer**: Peak season for offshore fishing, with warm waters attracting big game fish like tuna, mahi-mahi, and marlin. It's an excellent time for both trolling and deep-sea fishing.
- **Fall**: As waters cool, fishing can remain excellent, particularly for species like wahoo and sailfish. This season also brings fewer crowds, providing a more tranquil fishing experience.
- **Winter**: In tropical and subtropical regions, winter can still offer great fishing, especially for species that thrive in cooler waters, such as sailfish and certain types of tuna. However, winter storms can affect fishing conditions in some areas.

## Regional Variations

- **Tropical Regions**: Offer year-round fishing due to consistent warm water temperatures. Locations like the Caribbean, Southeast Asia, and parts of Australia are ideal for winter fishing trips.
- **Temperate Regions**: Have more defined fishing seasons, often influenced by migratory patterns and water temperatures. The U.S. East Coast, Europe, and Japan see significant variations in species

availability throughout the year.

- **Polar Regions**: Fishing seasons are short but can be highly productive, particularly for species adapted to cold waters. Locations such as Alaska and Norway are known for their robust seasonal fisheries.

## Choosing the Right Method for You
### Personal Interest

- **Thrill Seekers**: Sport fishing is ideal for those who love adventure and the challenge of catching big game fish.
- **Economic Goals**: Commercial fishing is suitable for individuals or families looking to make a livelihood from the sea.
- **Leisurely Pursuits**: Recreational fishing is perfect for those seeking relaxation and a connection with nature.

## Budget

- **High-End**: Sport fishing can be expensive due to the cost of specialized gear and charter services.
- **Moderate to High**: Commercial fishing requires significant investment in boats and equipment but offers potential returns.
- **Variable**: Recreational fishing can be done on any budget, from basic shore fishing to more elaborate offshore trips.

## Location

- **Coastal Areas**: Ideal for all types of offshore fishing due to proximity to rich fishing grounds.
- **Urban Centers**: Accessible recreational fishing options like charter services are available, though may require travel for sport or commercial fishing.
- **Rural Locations**: Often provide easy access to prime fishing spots and may have a strong tradition of commercial fishing.

By understanding the unique features of these top fishing locations and utilizing local tips and tricks, you can maximize your offshore fishing experience and increase your chances of landing the big one. Happy fishing!

# 5 - Targeting Specific Species

## Hook, Line, and Sinker

Picture this: Dave Johnson, a novice fisherman from Galveston, Texas, set out to enhance his fishing abilities one summer by trying to catch a shark. Dave was well-known for his experimental cooking style, creating amazing dishes using unexpected ingredients. However, he was better at cooking than fishing, so he got creative and used his leftover meatloaf as bait.

It was a sweltering July afternoon in 2005, and Dave had spent the morning preparing for his big fishing expedition. He meticulously checked his gear, ensuring his lines were strong and his hooks sharp. But when it came to bait, Dave realized he had forgotten to pick up the usual mackerel or squid. With the local bait shop closed for a holiday, Dave had to think fast.

As he rummaged through his cooler, he spotted the remains of the previous night's dinner—a hearty meatloaf wrapped in foil. Dave figured, "If it's good enough for dinner, it's good enough for the ocean.Despite his friends' confusion, he shaped the meatloaf around his hook, confident that its strong smell would lure a hungry shark.

Dave cast his line into the Gulf of Mexico with a confident flick of the wrist. The meatloaf bobbed in the water for a moment before beginning to disintegrate into a mushy mess. Undeterred, Dave stood at the edge of the boat, his friends snickering behind him. In just a few minutes, the warm Gulf waters dissolved his meatloaf completely, leaving only crumbs floating away.

No sharks were caught that day, but Dave's attempt became the stuff of local legend. His friends recounted the story with glee at every fishing outing, barbecues, and holiday gatherings. "Remember when Dave tried to catch a shark with meatloaf?" they'd laugh, shaking their heads in disbelief.

Despite the failed attempt, Dave's experiment served as a humorous reminder that not all baits are created equal. It underscored the importance of preparation and using the right tools for the job. Dave learned humility and the importance of laughter, both at himself and during fishing adventures. His story added depth to Galveston's fishing community, showing how anglers will do anything to catch the biggest fish.

## Profiles of Key Targets

**Marlin**

Marlin are prized for their size, strength, and spectacular fighting ability. These powerful fish can weigh over 1,000 pounds and are known for their long, spear-like bills and vibrant blue coloration.

**Tuna**

Tuna are fast-swimming predators found in warm waters worldwide. They are highly valued both commercially and recreationally, with species such as yellowfin, bluefin, and albacore being the most sought after.

**Grouper**

Groupers are robust bottom-dwellers known for their large mouths and strong bodies. They are commonly found in reefs and rocky areas, and some species can grow to over 500 pounds.

**Fresh Bait**

1. **Blue Marlin**: The largest blue marlin ever caught weighed 1,402 pounds and was landed off the coast of Brazil in 1992.
2. **Yellowfin Tuna**: Yellowfin can reach speeds of up to 50 mph, making them one of the fastest fish in the ocean.
3. **Goliath Grouper**: Historically known as jewfish, the goliath grouper can grow up to 800 pounds and has been protected from harvesting in U.S. waters since 1990.
4. **Swordfish**: These fish use their long, flat bills to slash at prey, stunning them before eating.
5. **Albacore Tuna**: Known as "chicken of the sea," albacore are valued for their mild flavor and high-quality meat.
6. **Black Marlin**: One of the largest and fastest marlins, capable of swimming at speeds up to 80 mph.
7. **Bigeye Tuna**: Bigeye are known for their large, expressive eyes and deep-water habitat, making them a challenging catch.
8. **Red Grouper**: These groupers are known for their bright red coloration and are a favorite target for both commercial and recreational fishermen.
9. **Sailfish**: Distinguished by their large, sail-like dorsal fin, sailfish can leap out of the water at speeds up to 68 mph.
10. **Mahi-Mahi**: Also known as dolphin fish, mahi-mahi are renowned for

their vibrant colors and acrobatic jumps when hooked.

11. **Pacific Bluefin Tuna**: These giants can grow up to 10 feet long and weigh as much as 1,500 pounds.
12. **Nassau Grouper**: Found in the Caribbean, this grouper is known for its striking pattern of dark bars on a light background.
13. **Striped Marlin**: Known for their beautiful stripes that are more vivid when the fish is excited or stressed.
14. **Dogtooth Tuna**: Not true tunas, these fish are related to bonitos and mackerels and are known for their ferocity.
15. **Gag Grouper**: A popular species for spearfishing, known for its robust, stout body and mottled appearance.
16. **White Marlin**: Smaller than blue and black marlins, but still a prized catch for sport fishermen due to their fighting ability.
17. **Skipjack Tuna**: Often used as bait for larger fish, skipjack are also valued for their light, flavorful meat.
18. **Warsaw Grouper**: One of the largest grouper species, capable of reaching weights over 400 pounds.
19. **Atlantic Bluefin Tuna**: A single Atlantic bluefin can fetch thousands of dollars, making it one of the most commercially valuable fish.
20. **Wahoo**: Known for their incredible speed and sharp teeth, wahoo are a favorite among anglers for their challenging fight and delicious meat.

## Best Practices for Each Target
### Marlin

- **Techniques**: Trolling with artificial lures or live bait.
- **Handling**: Use heavy-duty gear and a fighting chair to manage the marlin's strength. Avoid over-stressing the fish if planning to release.
- **Conservation**: Practice catch and release to help maintain marlin populations.

### Tuna

- **Techniques**: Chunking, trolling, and jigging are popular methods.
- **Handling**: Bleed tuna immediately after capture for best quality meat.

Use appropriate gear to handle their powerful runs.

- **Conservation**: Follow local regulations regarding size and bag limits to ensure sustainable tuna fisheries.

## Grouper

- **Techniques**: Bottom fishing with live or cut bait near reefs and wrecks.
- **Handling**: Use circle hooks to reduce injury, and avoid lifting large groupers by the jaw to prevent damage.
- **Conservation**: Observe closed seasons and protected areas to support grouper populations.

## Frozen Bait

1. **Swordfish**: Swordfish can dive to depths of over 2,000 feet, making them one of the deepest-diving fish.
2. **Mahi-Mahi**: The name "mahi-mahi" means "very strong" in Hawaiian, reflecting the fish's powerful fight.
3. **Atlantic Bluefin Tuna**: These tunas can cross the Atlantic Ocean in less than 60 days, showcasing their incredible stamina.
4. **Wahoo**: Wahoo have been known to reach speeds of up to 60 mph, making them one of the fastest fish in the sea.
5. **Pacific Bluefin Tuna**: These fish can migrate over 6,000 miles from Japan to the California coast in search of food.

**Case Studies and Success Stories**
**Marlin Mastery**
In 2018, angler Sarah Johnson from Melbourne, Australia, caught and released a record-breaking 1,200-pound black marlin off the coast of Cairns. Using a combination of live bait and expert trolling techniques, Sarah battled the marlin for nearly four hours before successfully bringing it alongside the boat for measurement and release. Her catch emphasized the importance of skill, patience, and adherence to conservation practices.
**Tuna Triumph**

Off the coast of Nova Scotia, in 2019, commercial fisherman Joe MacDonald landed a massive 1,000-pound bluefin tuna using traditional rod-and-reel methods. The catch fetched a high price at the Tokyo fish market, underscoring the commercial value of sustainable fishing practices. Joe's success was attributed to his deep knowledge of tuna behavior and his commitment to using environmentally friendly fishing gear.

**Grouper Glory**

In the Florida Keys, recreational angler Tim Baker achieved a personal best by catching a 400-pound goliath grouper in 2020. Tim used a combination of heavy tackle and live bait to entice the massive fish from its rocky hideout. The catch was documented and released, contributing valuable data to ongoing research efforts aimed at protecting this vulnerable species.

These stories highlight the incredible experiences and achievements that come with targeting specific offshore species. Whether it's the adrenaline rush of battling a massive marlin, the satisfaction of landing a prized tuna, or the sheer awe of encountering a colossal grouper, each species offers unique challenges and rewards.

By understanding the best practices for each target, utilizing high-tech gear, and respecting conservation efforts, you can enhance your fishing adventures and contribute to the sustainability of these magnificent marine creatures. So gear up, stay informed, and may your lines always be tight with the catch of your dreams. Happy fishing!

# 6 - Advanced Topics and Technology

**Hook, Line, and Sinker**

In July 2023, Kevin "Gadget Guru" Mitchell, a tech-savvy angler from Santa Monica, California, decided to revolutionize his fishing game with the latest technology—a state-of-the-art drone. Known for his innovative approach to everything from home automation to fitness tracking, Kevin was confident that his drone would give him a competitive edge in his offshore fishing adventures.

On a bright, sunny morning, Kevin set out on his boat, "The Silicon Sailor," armed with his drone equipped to carry and drop bait precisely where he wanted in the ocean. His friends had heard him brag about this ingenious plan for weeks, and today was the day he would prove them all wrong.

Kevin carefully programmed the drone, double-checked the settings, and with a proud grin, sent it soaring over the azure waters of Santa Monica Bay. Dangling below the drone was a juicy piece of bait, glistening in the sunlight. Everything seemed perfect. He envisioned the drone dropping the bait right into a school of fish, making for an easy and impressive catch.

However, Kevin hadn't accounted for one variable—Santa Monica's notoriously aggressive seagulls. As the drone hovered gracefully above the water, a flock of seagulls immediately spotted the dangling treat. Much to Kevin's horror and the seagulls' delight, they launched a coordinated aerial assault on the drone.

The scene quickly turned chaotic. Kevin watched in disbelief as his expensive gadget was swarmed by hungry birds, each one more determined than the last to snatch the bait. The drone struggled to stay steady as nature's unpredictability disrupted its precise programming.

Frantically, Kevin tried to maneuver the drone away from the frenzy, but it was too late. The drone, overwhelmed by the feathered attackers, managed to drop the bait—right into the middle of the seagull swarm, far from any fish. The seagulls made a lot of noise to celebrate their win, and Kevin's fancy plan failed in a funny way.

As Kevin retrieved his battered drone, the irony was not lost on him. His cutting-edge technology had been no match for the age-old cunning of seagulls.

The spectacle had drawn the attention of nearby boaters, who laughed and waved, shouting good-natured teases about his "genius" plan.

Kevin's high-tech fishing adventure quickly became the talk of Santa Monica Pier. His friends never let him forget the day nature had the upper hand, and Kevin learned a valuable lesson about the unpredictability of the great outdoors. Sometimes, despite our best efforts and the latest technology, nature still reminds us who's boss.

**Innovations and New Developments**
**Recent Innovations in Offshore Fishing Technology**

1. **Drone Fishing**: Drones are now used to scout for fish, drop bait, and even cast lines far beyond human capability.
2. **Smart Reels**: These reels feature digital displays showing line depth, water temperature, and fish activity, enhancing angler precision.
3. **Fish Finders**: Advanced sonar technology now provides detailed 3D images of the underwater environment, improving fish detection.
4. **Underwater Cameras**: High-definition underwater cameras allow anglers to monitor bait and fish behavior in real-time.
5. **Electric Reels**: Designed for deep-sea fishing, electric reels automatically adjust drag and retrieve line, reducing angler fatigue.
6. **Satellite Tracking**: Used in commercial fishing, satellite tracking devices monitor fish movements and ocean conditions.
7. **Biodegradable Lures**: Environmentally friendly lures made from biodegradable materials help reduce ocean pollution.
8. **Fishing Apps**: Apps like Fishbrain provide real-time data on fishing spots, weather conditions, and fish activity.
9. **Thermal Imaging**: Thermal cameras detect temperature changes in the water, identifying schools of fish.
10. **Autonomous Boats**: Autonomous, AI-powered boats can locate and follow fish without human intervention.
11. **LED Lures**: Lures equipped with LED lights mimic bioluminescent prey, attracting fish in deep or murky waters.
12. **Smart Rods**: Equipped with sensors, smart rods provide data on casting angles and fish bites.
13. **Wireless Fish Detectors**: These portable devices sync with

smartphones to display fish locations and water conditions.

14. **Artificial Intelligence**: AI algorithms analyze environmental data to predict fish behavior and optimize fishing strategies.

15. **Electric Outriggers**: These devices manage multiple lines and adjust to changing conditions, enhancing trolling efficiency.

16. **Virtual Reality (VR)**: VR training programs help anglers practice techniques and simulate fishing conditions.

17. **High-Strength Fishing Lines**: New materials like Dyneema offer superior strength and durability for deep-sea fishing.

18. **Portable Desalination Units**: These units provide fresh drinking water from seawater, essential for long offshore trips.

19. **Solar-Powered Gadgets**: Solar chargers keep fishing gadgets powered up during extended trips.

20. **Fish Handling Gloves**: High-tech gloves with grip-enhancing and cut-resistant features improve fish handling and safety.

# Fresh Bait

1. **Drone Fishing**: Originally used for aerial photography, drones have been adapted to deliver bait and spot schools of fish from above, revolutionizing the way anglers approach shore-based fishing. Early adopters in the 2010s pioneered these techniques, leading to widespread use today.

2. **Smart Reels**: Introduced in the early 2000s, smart reels now feature integrated GPS and data logging, allowing anglers to track their catches and improve their techniques. These reels help anglers monitor depth, speed, and environmental conditions in real-time.

3. **Side-Scan Sonar**: Developed during WWII for naval use, side-scan sonar is now a staple in fish finders, offering detailed images of the seabed and structures where fish might hide. This technology has greatly improved the accuracy and efficiency of locating fish.

4. **Biodegradable Fishing Gear**: To combat ocean pollution, companies have started producing biodegradable fishing lines and lures, reducing the impact of lost gear on marine environments. These eco-friendly products decompose naturally, minimizing long-term environmental

damage.

5. **LED Lures**: First used by commercial fishermen in the 1980s, LED lures have become popular among recreational anglers for their ability to attract fish in low-visibility conditions. These lures mimic bioluminescent prey, making them highly effective.

6. **Satellite Imagery**: Modern satellites provide real-time oceanographic data, helping fishermen locate prime fishing grounds by tracking sea surface temperatures and chlorophyll concentrations. This information aids in predicting fish migrations and feeding patterns.

7. **Virtual Reality Training**: VR systems allow anglers to practice their skills in simulated environments, enhancing their techniques before heading out to sea. These training programs offer realistic scenarios, improving preparation and confidence.

8. **Electric Outriggers**: These outriggers adjust automatically to optimize bait presentation and reduce tangles, making trolling more efficient. Introduced in the 2010s, they have since become a favorite among serious anglers.

9. **Autonomous Boats**: These AI-powered vessels can be programmed to scout for fish, providing real-time data to anglers on shore or in other boats. They represent a significant advancement in reducing human effort and increasing precision.

10. **Thermal Imaging**: Initially used in military applications, thermal imaging cameras are now helping fishermen detect fish by their body heat, even in complete darkness. This technology is especially useful for night fishing and in murky waters.

11. **Wearable Tech**: Devices like smartwatches and fitness trackers now come with fishing-specific apps that monitor weather conditions, track catches, and provide GPS navigation. These gadgets keep anglers connected and informed on the go.

12. **Fish Tracking Tags**: Researchers use electronic tags to monitor fish migrations, providing valuable data that helps commercial and recreational fishermen target specific species more effectively. This technology supports sustainable fishing practices.

13. **Hydrophone Technology**: Underwater microphones, or hydrophones, allow anglers to listen for fish sounds, helping locate

schools of fish that communicate via clicks and grunts. This acoustic monitoring can reveal hidden fish activity.

14. **Advanced Bait Systems**: Automated bait systems can dispense chum at regular intervals, attracting fish to a specific location for easier catching. These systems are particularly useful in commercial and sport fishing.

15. **Fish Aggregating Devices (FADs)**: Used by commercial fisheries, FADs create an artificial habitat that attracts fish, making them easier to locate and catch. They have been instrumental in increasing fish yields in open oceans.

16. **Biometric Fish Scales**: New scales can analyze the health and species of fish in real-time, providing valuable data for anglers and researchers alike. This technology enhances fish management and conservation efforts.

17. **Water Drones**: Submersible drones equipped with cameras and sensors explore underwater environments, providing real-time footage and data on fish movements and habitats. These drones offer a new perspective on underwater ecosystems and help locate fish more efficiently.

18. **Marine Weather Stations**: Portable weather stations provide real-time data on wind, waves, and atmospheric pressure, helping anglers make informed decisions about fishing conditions. These devices are crucial for safety and planning.

19. **Solar-Powered Boats**: Eco-friendly and efficient, solar-powered boats offer a sustainable alternative for offshore fishing, reducing fuel costs and emissions. These boats are becoming increasingly popular in the fishing community.

20. **Robotic Fish Attractors**: These devices mimic the movements and sounds of prey fish, attracting predators and improving catch rates. They represent a high-tech solution for enhancing fishing success.

## High-Tech Gear and Gadgets
### Reviews and Descriptions of High-Tech Gear

1. **Garmin Panoptix LiveScope**: This fish finder uses live sonar to

provide real-time 3D images of the underwater environment, making it easier to locate and track fish. Anglers can see detailed movements of fish and their reactions to lures in real-time.

2. **Deeper PRO+ Smart Sonar**: A portable, castable fish finder that syncs with your smartphone, offering detailed bathymetric maps and fish locations. Its compact size makes it perfect for shore, boat, or ice fishing.

3. **Shimano BeastMaster Electric Reel**: Ideal for deep-sea fishing, this electric reel features programmable settings and a powerful motor to handle large catches effortlessly. It reduces the physical strain of reeling in deep-water species.

4. **GoFish Cam**: An underwater camera that attaches to your fishing line, providing live video footage of the action below the surface. This device helps anglers understand fish behavior and improves bait presentation.

5. **Furuno NavNet TZtouch3**: A multifunction display system with advanced sonar, radar, and chart plotting capabilities for serious anglers. It integrates various navigation tools into one interface, enhancing fishing expeditions.

6. **Power-Pole Blade Shallow Water Anchor**: A remote-controlled anchor system that quickly and quietly secures your boat in shallow waters. It offers stability and precision positioning in depths up to 10 feet.

7. **Raymarine Axiom+**: A high-performance fish finder with quad-core processing and a super bright display for clear visuals in any conditions. It supports a wide range of sonar technologies and integrates with other marine systems.

8. **Tactacam Fish-i**: A versatile action camera designed specifically for fishing, with waterproof housing and mounting options for various setups. It captures high-quality video of your fishing adventures above and below water.

9. **Lowrance Ghost Trolling Motor**: A quiet, powerful trolling motor with integrated sonar and GPS capabilities, allowing precise boat control and positioning. Its brushless motor provides silent operation and long-lasting durability.

10. **Simrad NSS EVO3**: An advanced marine display offering superior

connectivity and integration with various fishing and navigation systems. It features a bright, sunlight-readable screen and robust chart plotting and sonar capabilities.

**Frozen Bait**

1. **Drone Fishing**: Some drones can carry and drop baits weighing up to 2 kilograms, expanding the reach of shore-based anglers significantly. They can cast lines up to 500 meters offshore.
2. **Fish Finders**: Modern fish finders can detect fish up to 3,000 feet below the surface, offering unparalleled depth exploration. They use sophisticated sonar technology to provide detailed underwater images.
3. **Electric Reels**: High-end electric reels can retrieve lines at speeds over 500 feet per minute, making deep-sea fishing less labor-intensive. These reels are particularly useful for catching large, deep-dwelling species.
4. **Underwater Cameras**: These cameras can provide footage in 4K resolution, allowing anglers to see underwater environments in stunning detail. They offer insights into fish behavior and habitat.
5. **Fishing Apps**: Apps like Fishbrain have over 10 million users worldwide, creating a vast community for sharing tips, locations, and catches. These platforms provide valuable data and foster a global fishing community.

**Future Trends**
**Predicting Future Advancements in Offshore Fishing Technology**

1. **AI-Enhanced Fishing Gear**: Artificial intelligence will continue to revolutionize fishing gear, from smarter fish finders that learn and adapt to better predicting fish movements based on environmental data. AI could provide personalized fishing strategies based on historical catch data.
2. **Advanced Biodegradable Materials**: As environmental concerns grow, expect more fishing gear made from biodegradable and eco-friendly materials, reducing the impact on marine ecosystems. These materials will decompose naturally without harming wildlife.

3. **Hyper-Accurate GPS Systems**: Enhanced GPS technology will offer even more precise tracking and mapping, helping anglers find and return to productive spots with pinpoint accuracy. These systems will integrate with other devices to create comprehensive fishing maps.

4. **Integrated Ecosystems**: Future fishing tech will see greater integration, with drones, smart rods, and fish finders all working together seamlessly to provide comprehensive data and enhance the fishing experience. This integration will make fishing more efficient and enjoyable.

5. **Enhanced Virtual Reality Training**: VR training programs will become more advanced, offering detailed simulations of various fishing environments and scenarios to help anglers refine their skills without ever leaving home. These programs will provide realistic practice in different conditions and locations.

The future of offshore fishing looks incredibly promising, with technology playing a crucial role in making the sport more accessible, efficient, and environmentally friendly. As innovations continue to develop, anglers will have more tools at their disposal to enhance their fishing adventures and connect with nature in new and exciting ways.

# 7 - Safety and Best Practices

**Hook Line and Sinker**

Tim "No Lifejacket" Thompson, a seasoned angler with a reputation for pushing the limits, decided to forgo his lifejacket on a seemingly perfect day off the coast of Key West. The sun was shining, the water was calm, and Tim, ever the confident swimmer, thought nothing could go wrong. He had fished these waters countless times and believed he knew every ripple and current.

Tim set out early that morning, reveling in the peaceful solitude of the open sea. With the engine humming softly and the gentle lapping of the waves against the hull, he felt invincible. As the hours passed, he hooked a few impressive catches, further boosting his already inflated confidence.

Around midday, without warning, a rogue wave—one of those rare and unpredictable giants—rose from the depths and slammed into his boat. Tim was thrown overboard in an instant, the world turning upside down as he plunged into the cold, unforgiving water. Panic set in as he surfaced, gasping for air, his boat now a distant silhouette.

Without his lifejacket, Tim quickly realized how helpless he was against the ocean's powerful currents. Each wave seemed to drag him further from his boat, and his strong swimming skills suddenly felt inadequate. He thrashed and struggled, trying to stay afloat, his energy draining with every desperate stroke.

Just as his strength began to fade, Tim spotted a fishing boat on the horizon. Mustering his last bit of energy, he waved frantically, hoping to catch the crew's attention. His heart pounded as he saw the boat change course and head towards him. Minutes felt like hours, but finally, the fishermen reached him, pulling him aboard to safety.

Exhausted and shivering, Tim lay on the deck, catching his breath and reflecting on his brush with disaster. The fishermen, seasoned veterans of the sea, gave him a stern lecture about the importance of safety gear. Tim nodded, chastened and grateful, realizing how close he had come to tragedy.

The lesson? No matter how calm the seas appear or how experienced you are, safety gear is non-negotiable. Tim's scary experience reminded everyone in the fishing community that the ocean can be dangerous, even though it looks beautiful and calm.

## Safety Guidelines and Precautions

1. **Life Jackets**: Always wear a life jacket when on the water. Even experienced swimmers can find themselves in dangerous situations.
2. **First Aid Kit**: Keep a well-stocked first aid kit on board, including items like bandages, antiseptics, and seasickness medication.
3. **Communication Devices**: Ensure you have reliable communication devices, such as a VHF radio and a backup satellite phone.
4. **Weather Check**: Always check the weather forecast before heading out. Sudden storms can turn a fishing trip into a hazardous adventure.
5. **Safety Drills**: Regularly conduct safety drills, so everyone on board knows what to do in an emergency.
6. **Emergency Position Indicating Radio Beacon (EPIRB)**: Carry an EPIRB to send a distress signal if you're in trouble.
7. **Float Plan**: File a float plan with a friend or family member detailing your trip's route and expected return time.
8. **Hydration and Sun Protection**: Bring plenty of water and sun protection gear, including hats, sunglasses, and sunscreen.
9. **Fire Extinguishers**: Ensure fire extinguishers are available and functional.
10. **Safety Harnesses**: Use safety harnesses when the weather is rough to prevent falling overboard.

## Fresh Bait

1. **First Lifejacket**: The first lifejackets, called "Mae Wests," were introduced during WWI and were named after the actress for their buoyant chest appearance.
2. **Early EPIRB**: The first EPIRB was developed in the 1970s, revolutionizing sea rescue operations by providing exact locations of distressed vessels.
3. **Marine VHF Radio**: Developed in the 1950s, VHF radios became essential for ship-to-shore communication, significantly enhancing maritime safety.
4. **International Distress Signal**: The SOS signal, adopted in 1906,

replaced the older "CQD" and became the standard distress signal worldwide.

5. **Automatic Identification System (AIS)**: Introduced in the early 2000s, AIS technology allows ships to see each other's movements, reducing collision risks.

6. **Weather Forecasting**: Modern weather forecasting, using satellites and computer models, began in the mid-20th century, vastly improving maritime safety.

7. **SOLAS Convention**: The International Convention for the Safety of Life at Sea (SOLAS) was established in 1914 after the Titanic disaster, setting safety standards for ships.

8. **Marine Fire Extinguishers**: First mandated in the 1920s, these devices have prevented countless onboard fires from becoming disasters.

9. **Helicopter Rescues**: The U.S. Coast Guard began using helicopters for sea rescues in the 1940s, significantly increasing survival rates.

10. **Sea Sickness Remedies**: Dramamine, introduced in the 1940s, provided a reliable way for sailors to combat sea sickness.

11. **Immersion Suits**: Developed in the 1960s, these suits can dramatically increase survival time in cold water.

12. **Flares**: Invented in the 19th century, pyrotechnic flares are crucial for signaling distress at sea.

13. **Emergency Liferafts**: Modern liferafts, required by SOLAS, are equipped with survival gear and are much more reliable than older versions.

14. **Personal Locator Beacons (PLBs)**: Introduced in the 1990s, PLBs can be carried by individuals and provide a personal distress signal.

15. **Anti-Collision Systems**: Radar, first used extensively in WWII, continues to be a vital tool for avoiding collisions at sea.

16. **Whistle Signals**: A tradition dating back centuries, specific whistle signals are used to communicate during rescues.

17. **Survival at Sea**: The "Survival at Sea" handbook, first published in the 1950s, is a critical resource for maritime safety.

18. **Life Rings**: These flotation devices have been standard equipment since the 19th century, offering a lifeline to those who fall overboard.

19. **Distress Flags**: Introduced in the early 20th century, these bright flags

signal distress to other vessels.

20. **Marine Safety Training**: Organizations like the Royal National Lifeboat Institution (RNLI), founded in 1824, provide crucial training and rescue operations.

## Ethical Considerations

1. **Catch and Release**: Practice catch and release to ensure fish populations remain healthy. Use barbless hooks to minimize injury.
2. **Limit Your Catch**: Only take what you need, respecting size and bag limits set by local regulations.
3. **Avoid Overfishing**: Be mindful of the species you're targeting and avoid those that are overfished or endangered.
4. **Respect Marine Life**: Handle fish and other marine life with care to minimize stress and injury.
5. **Eco-Friendly Gear**: Use gear that minimizes environmental impact, such as biodegradable lines and lead-free weights.

## Frozen Bait

1. **Lifejacket Use**: Studies show that 80% of boating fatalities could be prevented by wearing a lifejacket.
2. **Overfishing Impact**: Over 90% of the world's fish stocks are overfished or fully exploited, highlighting the need for sustainable practices.
3. **Marine Debris**: Fishing gear accounts for approximately 10% of marine debris, making the use of biodegradable materials crucial.
4. **Rescue Statistics**: The U.S. Coast Guard conducts over 15,000 rescue missions annually, underscoring the importance of safety precautions.
5. **Fish Survival Rates**: Catch and release practices can improve fish survival rates by up to 95% when done correctly.

## Environmental Impact

1. **Sustainable Fishing Practices**: Implementing sustainable fishing

practices helps preserve fish populations for future generations.

2. **Marine Protected Areas**: Support and respect marine protected areas designed to conserve marine biodiversity.

3. **Pollution Reduction**: Minimize pollution by properly disposing of trash and avoiding plastic waste.

4. **Bycatch Reduction**: Use techniques and gear that reduce bycatch to protect non-target species.

5. **Climate Change Awareness**: Stay informed about how climate change affects marine environments and adapt practices accordingly.

# 8 - A Tackle Box Full of Useless Trivia

**1. The Largest Bluefin Tuna Ever Caught**

The largest bluefin tuna ever recorded weighed an astonishing 1,496 pounds and was caught off the coast of Nova Scotia, Canada in 1979.

**2. Marlin Speed Demons**

Blue marlins are among the fastest fish in the ocean, capable of swimming at speeds up to 60 miles per hour.

**3. Oldest Fish on Record**

A Greenland shark was estimated to be over 400 years old, making it the longest-living vertebrate known to science.

**4. The World's Smallest Fishing Reel**

The world's smallest functioning fishing reel measures just 5 millimeters in diameter and was created by Japanese angler Takanori Shibata.

**5. Swordfish Diving Depths**

Swordfish can dive to depths of over 2,000 feet, allowing them to evade predators and hunt for deep-sea prey.

**6. Record-Breaking Swordfish Catch**

The heaviest swordfish ever caught weighed 1,182 pounds and was reeled in off the coast of Chile in 1953.

**7. Bigeye Tuna's Night Vision**

Bigeye tuna have large eyes that allow them to see in the dark, making them effective hunters in deep and low-light waters.

**8. Electric Reels for Deep-Sea Fishing**

Modern electric reels can retrieve lines at speeds over 500 feet per minute, reducing the physical strain of deep-sea fishing.

**9. The First Fish Finder**

The first electronic fish finder was developed by Lowrance Electronics in 1957, revolutionizing the way anglers locate fish.

**10. Marlin's Impressive Leaps**

Marlin are known for their acrobatic leaps out of the water, sometimes reaching heights of up to 10 feet.

**11. Mahi-Mahi Color Transformation**

Mahi-mahi can change color rapidly, flashing bright hues of blue, green, and yellow when excited or threatened.

## 12. The Most Expensive Tuna

A bluefin tuna sold for a record $3.1 million at a Tokyo auction in 2019, highlighting its value in the sushi market.

## 13. Bioluminescent Lures

Some modern fishing lures are designed to mimic bioluminescent prey, attracting fish in the dark depths of the ocean.

## 14. Fish Aggregating Devices (FADs)

FADs are used to attract fish by creating an artificial habitat in the open ocean, making it easier for anglers to locate schools of fish.

## 15. The Largest Fishing Net

The largest fishing net ever used was over 1.6 miles long and was employed by a commercial fishing vessel off the coast of Norway.

## 16. Tuna's Incredible Speed

Yellowfin tuna can swim at speeds up to 50 miles per hour, making them one of the fastest fish in the ocean.

## 17. Oldest Known Fishing Hook

The oldest known fishing hook, made from sea snail shell, was discovered in East Timor and is estimated to be 23,000 years old.

## 18. The First Fishing Rod Patent

The first patent for a fishing rod was granted in 1822 to Samuel Phillippe, a gunsmith from Pennsylvania.

## 19. Largest Grouper on Record

The largest grouper ever caught weighed 680 pounds and was landed off the coast of Florida in 1961.

## 20. Portable Fish Finders

Modern portable fish finders, like the Deeper PRO+, can be cast from shore and sync with smartphones, providing detailed underwater maps.

## 21. Trolling for Big Game

Trolling, a technique where bait is drawn through the water behind a moving boat, is particularly effective for catching large pelagic fish like marlin and tuna.

## 22. Record-Setting Kayak Fishing Trip

In 2014, angler Eric McDonald caught a 400-pound marlin from his kayak off the coast of Hawaii, setting a new world record.

### 23. The Heaviest Halibut

The heaviest Pacific halibut on record weighed 459 pounds and was caught in Alaska in 1996.

### 24. Ancient Chinese Fishing Reels

The first known use of fishing reels dates back to 4th century China, where they were used to store line rather than for casting.

### 25. The Penn Reel Legacy

Penn, a prominent reel manufacturer, has been a staple in the fishing industry since 1932, known for their high-quality saltwater reels.

### 26. Swordfish's Sword

Swordfish use their long, flat bills to slash at prey, stunning them before consumption, making them efficient hunters.

### 27. Circle Hooks' Conservation Role

Circle hooks are designed to hook fish in the corner of the mouth, reducing injury and increasing the survival rate of released fish.

### 28. Solar-Powered Fishing Gadgets

Solar-powered chargers and gadgets are becoming increasingly popular, offering sustainable energy sources for extended fishing trips.

### 29. Deep-Sea Lures

Some deep-sea fishing lures are equipped with LED lights and vibrating motors to mimic the movement and appearance of prey.

### 30. Kite Fishing Origins

Kite fishing, where baits are presented on the water's surface using a kite, was developed in China and is effective for targeting surface feeders.

### 31. The Largest Tarpon Caught

The largest tarpon ever recorded weighed 286 pounds and was caught off the coast of Guinea-Bissau in 2003.

### 32. Electric Outriggers

Modern electric outriggers adjust automatically to optimize bait presentation and reduce tangles, making trolling more efficient.

### 33. Warsaw Grouper Giants

Warsaw groupers can reach weights over 400 pounds, making them one of the largest grouper species in the ocean.

### 34. Atlantic Bluefin Tuna Migration

Atlantic bluefin tuna are known for their extensive migratory patterns, traveling thousands of miles across the ocean.

## 35. Fly Fishing in Saltwater

Saltwater fly fishing, which began gaining popularity in the 1960s, combines the skills of freshwater fly fishing with the excitement of offshore fishing.

## 36. Greenstick Fishing Technique

Originating in Japan, the greenstick fishing method uses long, flexible poles to suspend multiple lures, effectively targeting tuna.

## 37. Oldest Marine Sanctuary

The first marine sanctuary in the United States, the Monitor National Marine Sanctuary, was established in 1975 to protect the wreck of the USS Monitor.

## 38. Biometric Fish Scales

New biometric fish scales can analyze the health and species of fish in real-time, providing valuable data for anglers and researchers.

## 39. Fish Tracking Tags

Electronic tags used to monitor fish migrations provide crucial data that helps commercial and recreational fishermen target specific species more effectively.

## 40. Hydraulic Outriggers

Hydraulic outriggers extend fishing lines away from the boat, allowing for more lines to be trolled simultaneously, increasing the chances of a catch.

## 41. Longest Fishing Rod

The longest fishing rod on record measures 59 feet and 5 inches, crafted by fishing enthusiast Yumeji Himeno in Japan.

## 42. The "Chicken of the Sea"

Albacore tuna, often called "chicken of the sea," are prized for their mild flavor and high-quality meat.

## 43. World's Largest Fishing Tournament

The White Marlin Open, held in Ocean City, Maryland, is the world's largest billfish tournament, offering millions in prize money.

## 44. First Use of Sonar in Fishing

Sonar technology, initially developed for naval use during WWII, was first used in commercial fishing in the 1950s to locate fish schools.

## 45. Recreational Fishing's Economic Impact

Recreational fishing contributes over $125 billion annually to the U.S. economy, highlighting its significant economic role.

### 46. Catch and Release Conservation

The concept of catch and release in sport fishing emerged in the mid-20th century as a conservation effort to maintain fish populations.

### 47. The Alvey Reel Innovation

The Alvey sidecast reel, an Australian invention, is beloved for its simplicity and ruggedness, particularly suited for surf fishing.

### 48. Fish Finders with GPS Integration

Fish finders with integrated GPS systems, like the Garmin Panoptix LiveScope, offer precise tracking and mapping of fishing locations.

### 49. Spearfishing Competitions

Competitive spearfishing tournaments, showcasing the skills of divers worldwide, began in the mid-20th century and continue to grow in popularity.

### 50. Deep-Dropping Techniques

Deep-dropping, a technique that uses electric reels to fish at depths over 300 meters, has transformed deep-sea fishing by targeting species such as swordfish.

# Summary and Final Thoughts

As we reach the end of our deep dive into the world of offshore fishing, it's clear that this thrilling adventure is more than just a sport—it's a way of life. We've covered everything you need to know about offshore fishing, from gear and techniques to exciting stories of big catches. Each chapter has explored the captivating world of fishing, including gear, techniques, and our love for the ocean and its creatures.

Offshore fishing is filled with triumphs, lessons, and pursuing the perfect catch. The ocean remains a place of mystery and excitement, offering new challenges and opportunities with every outing. Whether you're a seasoned angler or a novice looking to cast your first line, the sea welcomes you to its endless adventure.

**Encouragement for Further Exploration**

The stories and knowledge shared in this book are just the beginning. The world of offshore fishing is vast and ever-evolving, with new techniques, technologies, and species to discover. We encourage you to continue your exploration, to venture out into the open water, and to create your own fishing tales. Share your experiences with fellow anglers, learn from each other's successes and mistakes, and contribute to the rich tradition of offshore fishing.

Every fishing trip is a chance to learn something new, to push the boundaries of your skills, and to forge unforgettable memories. So, grab your gear, set your course, and embark on your next offshore adventure. The ocean is waiting, and the stories are yours to make.

# References and Recommended Reading

For those who wish to delve deeper into the fascinating world of offshore fishing, here are some recommended books, articles, and resources:

**Books**

1. **"The Complete Guide to Offshore Fishing" by Bill Shedd**
   - A comprehensive guide covering techniques, gear, and species.
2. **"Offshore Pursuit: A Complete Guide to Blue-Water Sport Fishing" by John Unkart**
   - Detailed insights into targeting big game fish in offshore waters.
3. **"Saltwater Fishing Made Easy" by Dave Card**
   - Practical advice for both novice and experienced anglers.
4. **"The Fisherman's Ocean" by David A. Ross**
   - Understanding the ocean's dynamics to improve fishing success.
5. **"Big Game Fishing Journal: Tactics and Techniques" by Ken Schultz**
   - Advanced strategies for catching trophy fish.

**Articles**

1. **"The Science of Fish Finding" by Marine Electronics Magazine**
   - An exploration of modern fish-finding technologies.
2. **"Sustainable Fishing Practices" by Conservation International**
   - Best practices for sustainable and ethical fishing.
3. **"Deep-Sea Fishing Adventures" by Outdoor Life**
   - Stories and tips from seasoned offshore anglers.

**Online Resources**

1. **FishBase (www.fishbase.org[1])**
   - A comprehensive database of fish species worldwide.

---

1. http://www.fishbase.org

2. **The International Game Fish Association (IGFA) (www.igfa.org[2])**
   - Records, regulations, and resources for sport fishing enthusiasts.
3. **Saltwater Sportsman (www.saltwatersportsman.com[3])**
   - Articles, videos, and tips for offshore and saltwater fishing.

## Magazines

1. **Sport Fishing Magazine**
   - Monthly publication with articles on techniques, gear reviews, and fishing hotspots.
2. **Marlin Magazine**
   - Focused on big game fishing with tips, stories, and tournament news.

## Websites

1. **www.anglersjournal.com[4]**
   - In-depth articles and stories from the fishing community.
2. **www.boatus.com[5]**
   - Resources and tips for boating and fishing safety.

Thank you for joining us on this journey through the exhilarating world of offshore fishing. May your lines be tight, your catches be legendary, and your stories unforgettable. Happy fishing!

---

2. http://www.igfa.org

3. http://www.saltwatersportsman.com

4. http://www.anglersjournal.com

5. http://www.boatus.com

# Don't miss out!

Visit the website below and you can sign up to receive emails whenever Michael Clutton publishes a new book. There's no charge and no obligation.

https://books2read.com/r/B-A-IAFJB-WBKPD

BOOKS 2 READ

Connecting independent readers to independent writers.

Did you love *Offshore Fishing Adventures*? Then you should read *Echoes of Reality*[6] by Michael P. Clutton!

[7]

**Where digital dreams collide with reality, one AI's heart holds humanity's last hope.**In a future where virtual reality is indistinguishable from the real, Maya Brooks, a master hacker, navigates a digital universe teeming with danger and deceit. Alongside Alex Rodriguez, a fearless rebel leader, she uncovers a conspiracy designed to imprison humanity within this synthetic world. As they peel back layers of digital illusion, Gabriel, a mysterious AI with secrets that could shatter worlds, further complicates Maya's reality.Caught in a web of virtual and emotional entanglements, Maya faces choices that blur the lines between love and duty, machine and man. Her journey forces her to confront what it truly means to be human as she battles to thwart a catastrophic glitch that could trap souls in an eternal digital nightmare.Echoes of Reality invites readers into a vivid cyberpunk realm, where one AI's heart might be the key to salvation—or humanity's ultimate undoing.

---

6. https://books2read.com/u/baL9yL

7. https://books2read.com/u/baL9yL

Read more at www.mpcfiction.com.

# Also by Michael Clutton

**Hooked On Reel Fishing**
How to Tackle Saltwater Fishing
Big Game Fishing
Offshore Fishing Adventures

**The Juice Chronicles**
Bloodlines: The Juice Chronicles

**Your Great Big Grab Bag of Useless Helpful Tidbits**
Charity Giving Donation Revelation
300 Trashy Truths You Didn't Need to Know

Watch for more at www.mpcfiction.com.

# About the Author

Michael P. Clutton has been creating stories and art since he could hold a pencil. What began with cartoons and short fiction grew into a lifelong pursuit of finding the absurd, the heartfelt, and the quietly human in every idea he touches.

Known for his dry humor and wry take on life, Clutton blends imagination, wit, and emotional honesty across genres—from comedy and sci-fi to horror, literary fiction, and even the occasional tongue-in-cheek how-to guide. His work invites readers to laugh, think, and occasionally wince in recognition.

He lives in Southwest Florida with his wife, where inspiration comes as easily as the humidity. When he's not writing, he's probably drawing, fishing, or pretending his poker face still works.

Read more at www.mpcfiction.com.